Contents

Acknowledgements

This booklet has been collated with the support and advice of the members of the
Fortrose and Rosemarkie Local History Group
and residents of Fortrose and Rosemarkie
who have shared their memories and photographs.

Special thanks to Jenny Paterson, Hannah Alexander and Jackie Matheson for their contributions.

Photographs courtesy of
David Rendell
Hilary Aitchison
Groam House Museum
Fortrose and Rosemarkie Heritage

Photograph of Daniel Fraser (front cover)
courtesy of Jenny Paterson

1904 base map reproduced with the kind permission
of the Ordnance Survey

Thank you,

Chris Rendell
Chair, Fortrose and Rosemarkie Local History Group.
July 2013

ISBN: 978-1-905787-86-9

Printed by
For The Right Reasons
fortherightreasons@rocketmail.com

Introduction

There have been many changes to the shops and shopping along Fortrose and Rosemarkie High Streets over the last century.

Throughout the UK High Streets have lost their small independent shops to the out of town retail park and now the internet online shopping is threatening the continued existence of the 'High Street' as we have known it. Rosemarkie has lost 80% of its shops since 1900 while Fortrose is surviving quite well having lost only 40%.

Although Rosemarkie is the older of the two settlements there has historically been more opportunities to prosper in Fortrose since Bishop Robert the Elder moved his Palace and Cathedral to the hamlet of Chanonrie some time in the thirteenth century. Chanonrie became the Royal Burgh of Fortrose in 1590.

In both Rosemarkie and Fortrose the nature of retailing has changed. Shops that serve the local population with their everyday needs stand alongside those that cater for both the day visitor and the caravan-staying holidaymaker.

Before the watershed of the First World War the better-off families like the Mackenzies and the Fowlers had always been accustomed to import quality goods, like furniture or clothes and fine wines, from Edinburgh or London. As farmers grew wealthier through improved farming practices, there was a growing demand for superior agricultural implements and machinery beyond the capacity of the local blacksmith.

Local people have always travelled into Inverness for special items. A shopping trip to Inverness by bus or train in the first half of the twentieth century would have been a whole day expedition. Ladies no doubt looked forward to a visit to town where they could dress up to see and be seen. High quality, personal service was the priority then so a lady's purchases would be delivered to the railway station by the 'boy' to be picked up on the way home.

A time traveller from the past would be amazed at today's brightly lit, colourful shop interiors with their wide range of branded goods on display. But they might wonder where was the chair for a lady to sit on while she made her purchases and regret the limited opportunity for conversation with friends and neighbours.

Today's time traveller going back to 1900 might have difficulty recognising which premises were the shops since many were still just a front room in a house or indistinguishable from a workshop. The first purpose built shop in Rosemarkie, 'Steavenson's General Merchants' of the mid 1800s, became Hugh Home's 'High Class Grocery' then Mary Ann MacGillivray's 'Store'. It is now a private home, 'Doric House'.

The late Victorian era saw a boom in the construction of purpose built shops throughout the whole country. The development of plate glass in 1834 meant that shop windows increased in size to maximise light and could be used to display goods. In Rosemarkie, Dornkop was built as a detached house and shop in the 1890s. Dornkop, built with money from South Africa, went on to house William Robb's 'Cash Grocery' and Daniel Fraser's 'D. & G. Fraser Grocers' (see front cover) then Mrs Jones' 'Shoe Shop'. Today it is the home of 'Panacea'.

Stuart's 'Grocery and Drapery' claimed, in an advertisement in the Ross-shire Journal, to be the oldest shop in Fortrose and appears in the 1881 Census. Stuart's may well have been the first purpose built shop on the High Street but the 1871 census, however, shows John Smith, Clothier, open for business in Union Street. John Smith later had a Draper's shop on the High Street itself, opposite Cathedral Antiques.

Stuart's continued to be a retail outlet until 2012 but the nature of the shop and its business changed through the years and reflects the overall pattern of shopping both nationally and on the Black Isle. From being a draper/grocer/general merchant, selling a comprehensive range of goods it became a grocery store and then a MACE supermarket. Finally, meeting the needs of the visitor rather than local residents it became a Belgian Chocolatier's.

A Century of Shopping along Fortrose High Street

Fortrose is an attractive small town on the Black Isle. Once a small hamlet on the Chanonry peninsula in the parish of Rosemarkie it owes its prominent position to the building of the Cathedral there in the thirteenth century. Fortrose became the focus of ecclesiastical affairs with the parishes of the Black Isle represented in the manses that surrounded the Cathedral building. Following the Reformation and the destruction of the Cathedral, Fortrose continued to be a popular place of residence for annuitants and pensioners, a practice that persists to this day.

The building of the Telford harbour in the early 1800's consolidated Fortrose's prosperity as a market town with a weekly Wednesday market and three annual fairs. The town was linked to Inverness, Aberdeen and London in the 1840's by the weekly steamer, 'Northern Star' and was in a unique position to serve the commercial and industrial needs of the locality. When the coastal shipping trade began to decline, the town's importance was maintained by the opening of the Highland Railway branch line in 1894 linking Fortrose to Inverness and Dingwall.

Fortrose had a well-established commercial base along the High Street by 1900. There were purpose built shops supplying a variety of products and services like the Post Office as well as the Caledonian Bank. For many towns and villages the First World War was a watershed with few shops surviving the price rises and shortages of the war years and the problems created by the Depression that followed. Fortrose's unique position, fertile farmland, geographically attractive with rolling hills and rocky coastline and still so socially acceptable that incomers were attracted into the town, meant that the High Street continued to thrive.

The low point in Fortrose's shopping history came in the last quarter of the twentieth century when many shops closed. The opening of the Kessock Bridge in 1982 improved access to the superior retail opportunities of Inverness and the local shops could not compete. The town kept its essential shops, the bakery, the butcher and the Co-operative Store many others were turned into storage or offices.

Then in 1986 Mr and Mrs Alexander decided to retire and the bakery closed. There had been a bakehouse and bakery at 45 High Street from the 1870's. It was symbolic of the trade craftsmen who had served their community and a link with the past had been broken. The shop stood empty for some time until it was taken over by the new type of shop to rejuvenate the High Street, 'Cathedral Antiques'.

This antique shop and the 'Fat Frog' coffee bar in 'The Studio Jewellery Workshop', appeal to a different sort of customer, the leisure shopper, who comes to Fortrose for a relaxing experience as part of a holiday to see the dolphins at Chanonry or visit the Cathedral for the annual St Boniface Fair. But the High Street has been rejuvenated and the local customers still have their butcher, two new baker's shops and a chemist.

Follow the stories of these shops past and present,
using the ***History Trail*** along the High Street.

Start the trail by the Union Tavern and walk as far as the
Co-operative Supermarket.
Then cross over the road and walk back to the site of the Mercat
Cross and end the trail by enjoying refreshment in the
Eilean Dubh Restaurant.

Look carefully for the sheaf of wheat on the gable end of the bakery. If you are very observant you may find evidence of John Smith's 'clothier's' shop. A useful indicator of previous use as a shop is an extra large window next to a door in a private house.

A Century of Shops and Shopping
History Trail

Fortrose High Street

23 High Street **Bank of Scotland**
Formerly the Caledonian Bank. The Agent and his family lived above the bank.

27 High Street (now a private house)
Alexander McIver, *Shoemaker* appears in the 1901 Census but has gone by 1911, Slater's Trade Directory.

The Union Tavern
The 1901 census records Margaret Smith as the spirit dealer living with her son Simon, a tailor and her niece, Mary Young who was a dressmaker.

The Union Tavern

The **Union Tavern** was one of several 'tippling houses'. There was also 'The Ship Inn', Academy Street, 'Fraser's Arms', Main Street (now High Street), 'The Grapes', North Street and the 'White Horse' at Chanonry Point.

Tavern House site
Murdoch Matheson, *Grocer, Baker and Tea Rooms*

Murd described himself as a 'grocer, provisions merchant, baker and confectioner'. In the 1930s Murd sold butter, sugar, black and white puddings (Val Roll 1931-39). He was a bit of a joker too. Once when he suspected someone of pinching the occasional black pudding, he tied all the black puddings together so that the next time this person tried to slip one into her pocket, a trail of black puddings followed her out of the grocery shop.

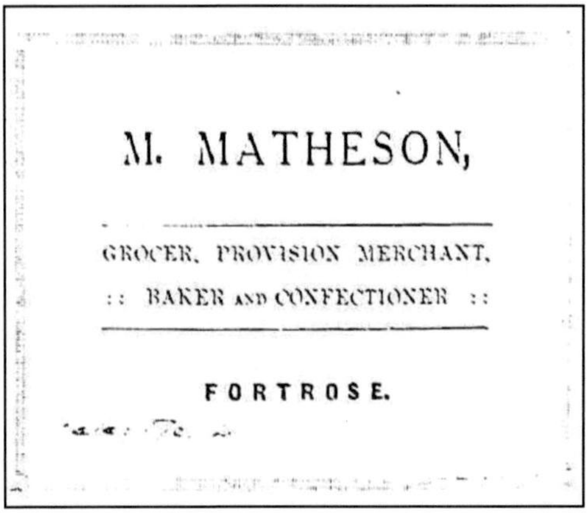

Murdoch Matheson's advert in the North Star (1930)

Murd Matheson also ran a grocery/bakery shop at 49 High Street for a short time. Murd was still in business next to the Tavern in 1955/6 (Val Roll).

The Home family who ran the High Class Grocery in Rosemarkie owned several properties between the Union Tavern and Cathedral
Antiques in the first half of the twentieth century.

The only shop remaining is **Harry Gow, *Bakers*.**
This shop opened about 2007.

31 High Street
James McKeddie
This was a **café** for a short time, mid 20th century, run by the McKeddie family (Val Roll 1960,65/6).

33 High Street (now a private house)
James Wilson, *Plumber* rented the property from Helen Bates Home in the 1930's. He lived at Clematis Cottage.
Roddy Sangster, *Plumber* displayed plumbing accessories and sanitary ware here. Valuation Roll 1955/56, 1965/66 1971/2. Roddy Sangster also owned a store and workshop down at the Shore. By 1985 number 33 was used as a store only.

Ferrier, *Greengrocer*

35 High Street
(now a private house)
Ray and Pat Ferrier, *Greengrocer*
In the 1970's, the Ferriers sold fruit and vegetables but by 1985 it was used only as a store.

37 High Street (now a private house)
James Munro, Butcher is recorded in the 1901 Census and 1903 Slater's Trade Directory employing his wife Mary and a young man, John McIntosh.

39 High Street (now a private house)
In 1935/6 the property was owned by **R.Home,** the ***Blacksmith*** on the Shore. **Alex Duncan, *Barber*** had his barber shop there in 1971/72 before moving to the back of the chemist shop on Station Road.

43/45 High Street

Cathedral Antiques

For most of their life these premises have been used as a bakery, baker's shop and tea rooms.

James Fraser had a **bakery** with Alexander Anderson, foreman baker living above the shop (1901 Census). James Fraser's wife worked in the baker's shop and was known by the bi-name of Mrs Bappy after the baps she sold.

When James Fraser retired he sold the business to **Harold Alexander**, who advertised his **Bakery** and tearooms in the North Star. Declaring that 'Fortrose and Rosemarkie For Good Weather and Lovely Surroundings' the advert recommends a visit to Alexander's for 'Good Food—Best Bread, Cakes and Confections'

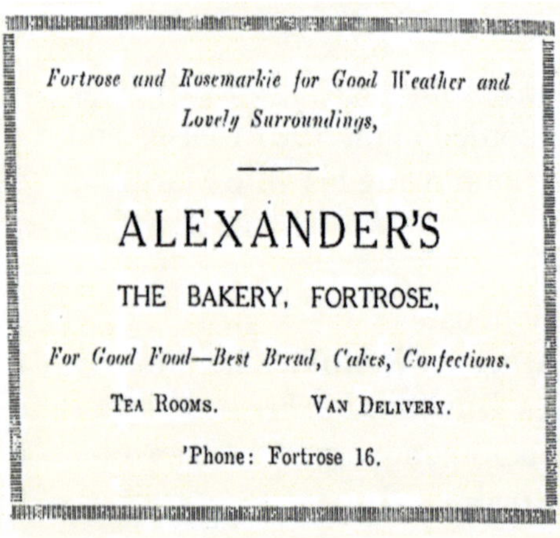

Harold Alexander's advert in the North Star (1930)

Thomas Johnston Ure
Bakers and Tea Room
took over the bakery and tea rooms in 1935 until after the Second World War.

Mr A.A.Alexander and his wife, Hannah
(no relation to Harold) rented the bakery from 1946 onwards.

Alexander's Bakery

Alexander Alexander started work in the bakery at 2.00am so that Hannah Alexander had bread ready to sell when the shop opened at 9.00am. The baker specialised in small rough loaves, milk loaves and bread rolls. Coming from the other side of the Moray Firth he was particularly noted for his Wine biscuits, a speciality of the Moray coast and similar to modern butter biscuits.

Mr Alexander also enjoyed decorating any wedding cakes requested and was happy to display them in the bakery.
By the late 1980s the Alexanders had retired and the shop stood empty for several years until taken over by Cathedral Antiques who sell a range of antiques.

Hannah Alexander with the late Catherine Wilson and Eve Taylor. Hannah and her staff in traditional baker's outfits, selling their popular biscuits and cakes at the annual St Boniface Fair in the late 1980s.

(left) Hannah Alexander

47 High Street

Boots the Chemist

This has always been a pharmacy/chemist/druggist. At the beginning of the 20th century the druggist was **James Robertson**. By the 1930s the proprietor of the 'Black Isle Pharmacy' was
James Gow.

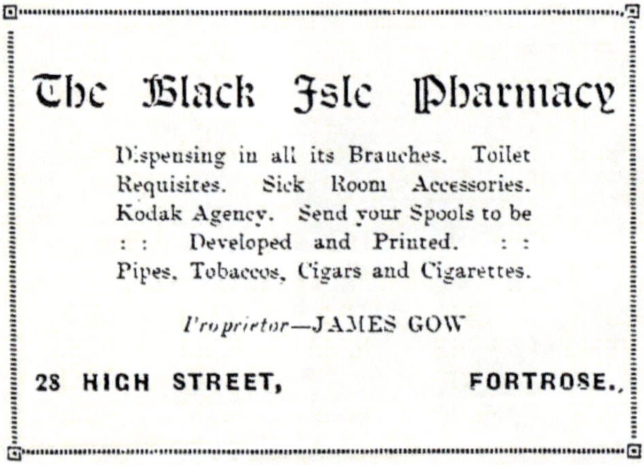
The Black Isle Pharmacy

Dispensing in all its Branches. Toilet Requisites. Sick Room Accessories. Kodak Agency. Send your Spools to be : : Developed and Printed. : : Pipes, Tobaccos, Cigars and Cigarettes.

Proprietor—JAMES GOW

28 HIGH STREET, FORTROSE.

Black Isle Pharmacy Advert, North Star (1930)

Angus Gow joined his father some years later to not only dispense medicines but also to sell toilet requisites, sick room accessories, pipes, tobacco, cigars and cigarettes.

The Pharmacy also acted as a Kodak Agency to develop and print photographs in that pre-digital age when everybody used film. Angus Gow was a keen photographer and displayed pictures of local events and weddings in the shop.

It was still 'Gow the Chemist' in 1985 but by 1995 there was a new chemist, **Mohammed Shafi**.

There used to be a 'dole' office outside, in Station Road, where young men went to register for the army.

The Chemist's shop opposite John Smith's Clothiers

49 High Street

The sheaf of wheat plaque on the front wall of this shop tells us it started out as a Bakery and although still a baker's shop today there have been many changes over the century of shopping.

Cromarty Bakery

In 1911 the **baker** was **John Macleod**. After John's death, Mrs Macleod rented the shop and bake house to Murdo Matheson, the baker/grocer next to the Union Tavern.

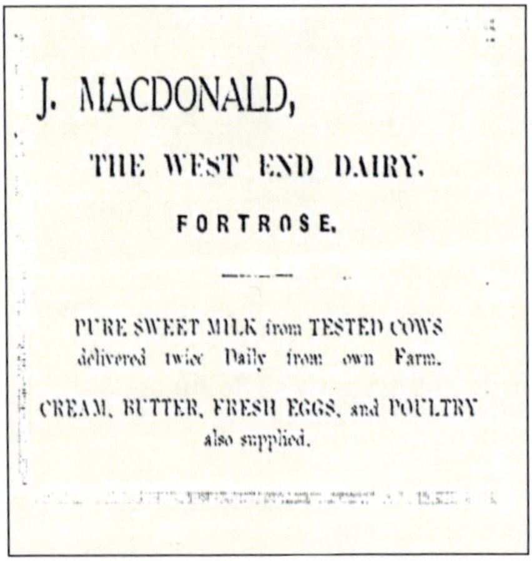

John Macdonald took over in the 1930s and renamed the business **'The West End Dairy'.** The dairy sold 'pure sweet milk from tested cows' as well as cream, butter, fresh eggs and poultry.

Macdonald's advert

John's brother, Tom Macdonald, had a dairy farm under the railway bridge at the top of Bishop's Road and he delivered milk from a van or you could take your own pail to the farm to be filled.

Tom Macdonald's Farm overlooking Fortrose from the ridge above the railway

In the late 1930s, Dorothy Kate Macdonald's father**,** **Kenny Macdonald**, had it as a **bakery** again.
George Brooks rented it for his **electrical business** in 1946.
Dorothy Kate Haytor (nee Macdonald) inherited the family home but the shop stood empty in the 1950 and 60s.

More recently it was **Ina Anderson's** ***Hairdressers*** (1970s), a private residence, then for several years in the last two decades of the twentieth century, it was the office of the **Highlands and Islands Fishermen's Association**.
Recently it was briefly the **'Farm Shop'** and now since 2010, it is a shop outlet for **'The Cromarty Bakery',** all the bakery being done in Cromarty.

51 – 61 High Street

Library Buildings and Victoria Buildings are now private houses but the Valuation Rolls and Trade Directories show several have been used as shops over the century of shopping

John Fraser, *Tailor*
John Fraser's tailoring business is recorded in the 1901 Census and Slater's Trade Directory for 1903 and 1911.

Mrs McLennan, *Fancy Goods*
The Inland Revenue Survey, 1911, records this as a fancy goods shop probably including sales of stationery.
Much later, we find **Dorothy Brooks** running a ***hairdressing salon*** (1971/72). Dorothy Brooks' husband, **Ross Macdonald** had an ***Electrical*** shop there.

A.R.Ross (1971/72)
The Valuation Roll records only that the shop was owned by Mrs Smith. There is no information on what was sold there. Later Mrs Smith acted as a collecting agent for the payment of bills.

George Munro, *Shoemaker*
Charles Macandrew, *Shoemaker*
Charles MacAndrew is recorded as living at 'Loandhu'.

There were several shoemaker or boot makers in Fortrose at the beginning of the 20th century. Slater's Directory 1911 and the Census for 1901 list John Ross, Donald Ross, Andrew Paton, Thomas Ross, Alexander Fraser, Alexander McIver, George Davidson and Donald McDonald as boot and shoemakers.

Hannah Alexander remembers George Munro and Charles MacAndrew as shoemakers in the 1930s. Both men had lost a leg and took up shoemaking in rehabilitation.

GEORGE MURRAY,

CONFECTIONER AND TOBACCONIST.

FORTROSE.

George Murray ,
Stationer
Val Roll 1931/2
Miss Alex Murray,
Stationer
Val Roll 1938/9

Alexander Watson, *Barber*

Alexander Watson, ***Barber*** rented 'Loandhu' from Charles MacAndrew during the Second World War (Val Roll 1942/3).

The red and white pole which used to be outside Victoria Buildings, is the traditional sign for a barber/surgeon.

Find the building (opposite the 'Anderson') by the style of window on either side of the double door.

61 High Street

John M. Munro, ***Butcher***

This appears to have been a butcher's shop for many years. The present butcher is John M Munro, a local butchery chain.

It was **Harpers the *Butchers*** before it was taken over in the 1960s by **John Butchart, *Butcher.*** After Butcharts left, **Sandy Jack** took over the business, running it successfully for some forty years (Valuation Roll 1971/2,85,95).

Sandy Jack, *Butcher*

Kate Evans, Jack Stuart's daughter, is said to have had had a toy shop here in the 1930s, next door to her father's establishment at number 63 but there is no record of this in the Valuation Rolls so perhaps she just had a corner in her parent's shop .

63 High Street

This imposing building was originally **John Stuart's *Grocery and Drapery.*** The Stuarts claimed to be the oldest shop in Fortrose and appear on the 1881 Census but John Smith, a Draper was listed in 1871 although not on High Street. Jack Stuart ran the grocery part while his wife had the drapery section.

The oldest shop in Fortrose

Stuart's advert in the North Star

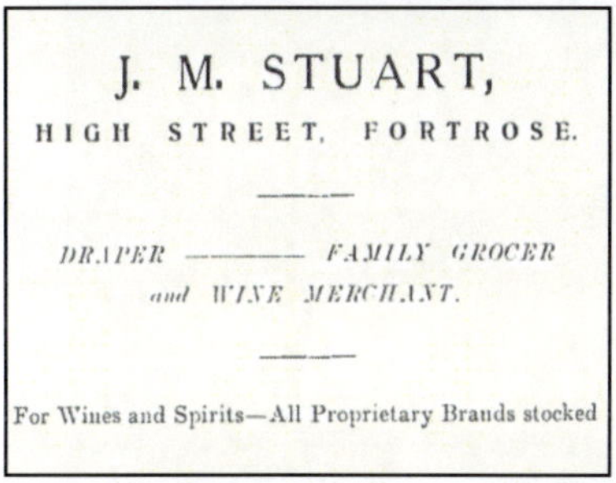

By the 1930s they were describing themselves as 'draper, family grocer and wine merchant' stocking 'all proprietary brands'. Stuart also arranged holiday lettings in and around Fortrose. Orders were both collected and delivered to customers.

In the late 1950s the Stuart's business was taken over by **Jessie Maclean** who sold it on to **Alex Young, *Grocer.***
Alex was better known as a footballer. He came from Aberdeen to play football for Ross County 1958-65. Mr and Mrs Young were still in Fortrose as a traditional family grocers in 1972.

After the Youngs left the building stood vacant or was used as a store in the 1980s and 90s until once again a grocery store it became the **MACE supermarket**.

Then finally, the Belgian Chocolate shop, before closing in 2012.

65 High Street (demolished)

John Grigor, *Draper*

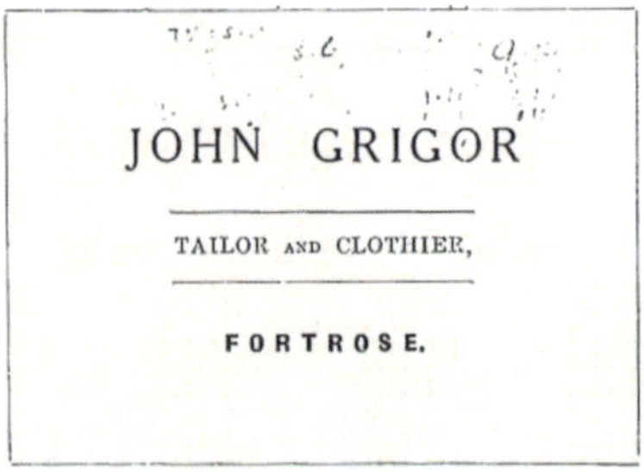

John Grigor is recorded in Slater's Trade Directories in 1903/11. By the 1930s he is advertising himself as a 'Tailor and Clothier'. The building was demolished post war to improve motor access into Church Street.

67/69High Street

The Co-operative Stores

There was a shoemaker and a tailor here before the First World War. Old **Donald Nelson** from Glasgow repaired bicycles in the house/shop behind 'Viewfort House', 67 High Street.

Rory Mackenzie expanded his business in the 1930s from his ***flesher's*** across the road (at 40 High Street) to include a ***butcher's*** shop run by his wife at 67 High Street.
His family including his daughter, Hannah Alexander formerly Mackenzie, lived above 'Viewfort House'.

67/69 High Street

By 1955 **George Brooks** had moved his ***'Electrical Store'*** here. George Brooks had rented premises in various places along the High Street and in Castle Street before he purchased Viewfort House. The Valuation Roll 1971/72 records the Electrical Shop and Store as being run by his son, **David Brooks**.

In the 1980s **Mario Pagliari** ran an ***off licence*** from number 67 while David Brooks continued at number 69. The buildings were part demolished in 2001 for the Co-operative Stores to relocate from further up the High Street. The present site includes car parking space.

Andrew Paton, Bootmaker

On the other side of the High Street, at the junction with Castle Street, **Andrew Paton, *Bootmaker*** had a shop and workshop. Andrew Paton is recorded in the Census 1901 and continued until at least 1932 according to the Valuation Roll.
Like John Grigor's opposite, the building was demolished post war to improve vehicular access to Castle Street/High Street.

42 High Street (now a private house)
Robert Miller, ***Flesher*** had his butcher shop here in 1911 before moving to The Cross.
William Mackenzie, ***painter*** rented this property in 1938/9. For many years after the Second World War it was **Sammy Munro**, ***Shoemaker's*** home and workshop until he moved to a new workshop (1960s) on Station Road. In the 1800's Fortrose was famed for its many shoemakers with premises in and around the High Street.
Sammy Munro was the last shoemaker in Fortrose .

His **'SHOEMAKER'** signpost can still be seen on the corner wall of Boots the Chemist's shop.

40 High Street
Roderick known as Rory, Mackenzie, ***Flesher***
Rory Mackenzie wintered sheep at Craiglands and had some sheep at Tomatin. Hannah Alexander nee Mackenzie remembers their shepherd lodger (Val Roll 1909,14,1939).

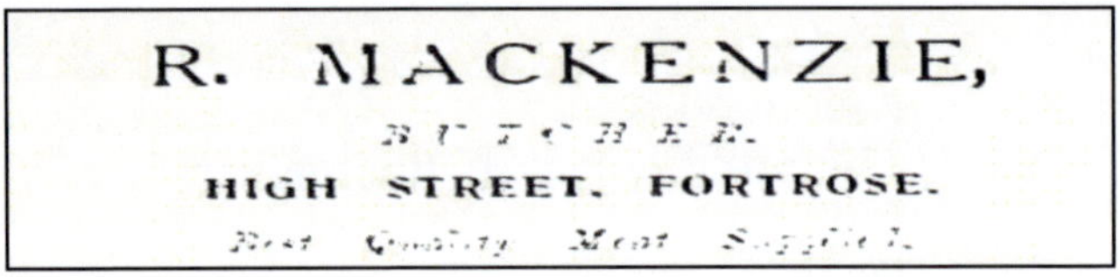

This building was later owned by **Alexander Wilson 'Dodo',** the ***Plumber*** and used as a store but by 1995 it was uninhabitable.
Dodo Wilson, the plumber, had a showroom for sanitary wares next door at number 42, until the mid 1990s

38 High Street

In the 1930s Fortrose was a popular holiday destination so there were several cafes and tea rooms like **Margaret Rennie's Restaurant** serving breakfasts, luncheons and teas at moderate' prices.
Indeed Mrs Rennie is listed as running 'refreshment rooms' at number 38, as early as 1911.
Mrs Rennie also sold sweets and Hannah Alexander remembers buying 'pandrops' a sort of acid drop sweet from her.

McGinty, ***Fish and chips***

RENNIE'S RESTAURANT

BREAKFASTS — LUNCHEONS — TEAS

MODERATE.

Just before the Second World War the **Pagliari family**, Enrico, then Charlie and later his nephew Mario and wife, Carla, opened the **'Merrythought Café'**. They sold delicious Italian ice cream and sweeties from big jars (Val Roll 1938,65,95). They maintained the business to the end of the century.

Then it became a series of fish and chip shops with several different owners before **McGinty** successfully took it over in 2005.

The Anderson

There has long been a 'hotel' or 'public house' here but it has been known by various names. In the Slater's Trade Directory of 1911 **Walter Grant** is named as host at the **'Royal Station Hotel'**.

In 1911 the Hotel had 2 dining rooms and 3 public rooms on the ground floor with a further 2 public rooms upstairs. There were 16 bedrooms. Out back there were two stable blocks one catering to 5 horses and the other 6 horses. There was also a harness room, byre, and turnip shed.

The Anderson

In more recent times it has been known as 'The Anderson after its American owner, **Jim Anderson**. The Anderson is known for the wide range of whiskies sold there.

Mackerchar Drill Hall **Picture House**

The Volunteer Drill Hall was built in 1881 by John Robertson and was still in use as a drill hall for First World War volunteers. It was very popular from the 1930s onward as a cinema. Pictures were shown Monday, Wednesday, Friday and Saturday. Queues would stretch down as far as Hugh Penney's house, 'Springfield'. It would be a packed house for films showing George Formby or Laurel and Hardy.
Lyall Hunt and Jimmy Lumsden showed the films.

It was also put to good use for fancy dress balls at Christmas. The Fancy Dress Dance, Christmas night, 1930, the Master of Ceremonies was Bert Miller the butcher from the Cross.
It was also used for concerts and sport. Many Fortrose residents have fond memories of its use as the school gym.

Drill Hall and Garden of Remembrance

32 High Street

The Post Office

The Post Office moved to its present location at 32 High Street when the postmaster, John Protheroe, retired from number 24, further along the High Street.
This building has seen many changes. In the 1901 census it was home to Dr William Maclean who held his surgery there. Twenty years later it was the family home of the Ross family who were drapers.

32 High Street

Isabella or Isa Ross described herself as a ***'Draper'***. She is recorded in the Valuation Roll in 1931 and Isa Ross was still selling wool and baby clothes in the late 1960s (Val Roll 1931 – 1965).

Then a **Mr Moyes** had it as a ***Draper's*** selling jumpers and knitting wool.

Leslie Smith opened **Fortrose Hardware Store** on the High Street in 1980, following the closure of 'West End Stores' on Canonbury Terrace at the top of St Andrew's Walk. He was still running the Hardware store at the end of the century and lives nearby in Cathedral Square, Fortrose.

30 High Street (now a private house)

You can still read the shadow 'tailor' 'clothier' written above the door which is the **John Smith**, ***Draper***, of Slater's Trade Directory, 1911

John Smith, Tailor and Clothier

John Smith owned several properties including two shops and his own house in Academy Street. By the 1930s John Smith was dead and his High Street property was under much needed repair.

28 High Street (now a private house)

The OS map (1904 edition) records a **Post Office** here. **Ann Mackenzie** was ***Assistant at the Post Office*** (1901 Census). Later **Mackenzie, *Jeweller*** (Mrs Mackenzie. Widow, Val roll 1931-39). It is not known who was the jeweller in the family.

Mr **Jan Baginski, *Watchmaker*** occupied these premises after the Second World War. He was a Polish man who had settled here rather than return to Poland. His house had a door onto the High Street and his workshop for mending clocks and watches was in one of the front rooms.

The Fat Frog in the Exchange Building

Now a jewellery and tourist type gift shop, 'The Studio Jewellery Workshop' this used to be a much-frequented local shop. It is an imposing building with the Institute above.

Previously this had always been a Grocer/Draper shop. At the beginning of the 20th century it belonged to **William Geddies**. The Geddies family lived there and his daughter, Elizabeth was a shop assistant. Sometime in the 1920s the property was taken over by **E.R.Anderson**. Ebenezer Readie Anderson sold the 'finest Belfast hams', 'Ayrshire Roll' bacon and 'Wiltshire' bacon. He also sold drapery and hardware and acted as an agency for Pullar's of Perth (Valuation Rolls 1931 to 1939).

E. R. Anderson's Advert in the North Star (1930)

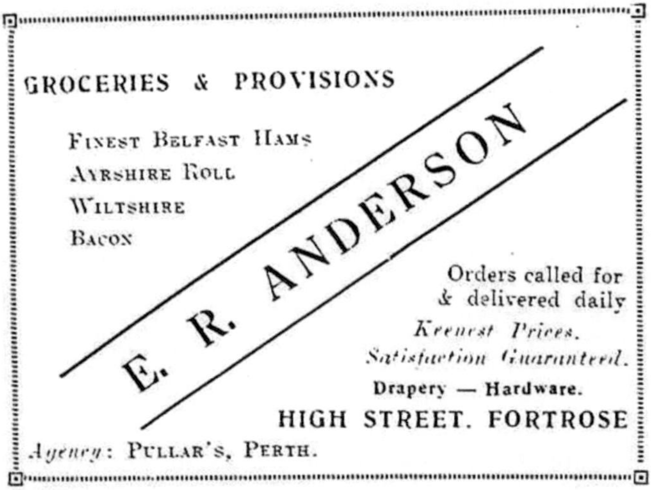

Allan B Ramsay ran a **General Merchant's** here during the Second World War.

This shop was to be Fortrose's first 'chain' store when it was taken over by the SCWS in 1946 The **Co-operative Store** sold almost everything. There was a drapery department as well as the grocery store.

Members of the Co-op had a number so that they could claim their dividend. 'It was something you had to remember. When you made a purchase, the assistant wrote your number on a slip of paper for you to keep.' This was proof of entitlement to dividend, a payout from the Co-op based on how much you had spent. Local shoppers commented that prices seemed to be much more stable in those days.

The Co-op was also the first to become a self-service shop in Fortrose. You served yourself to the pre-packed goods on the shelf and went to the till near the exit to pay for them.

The Fat Frog

The SCWS Co-operative Store moved to a purpose built self -service supermarket in 2001 at 67/69 High Street. The Co-operative store continues to serve the local community today.

Highland Podiatry Services

Dorothy Kate MacDonald who married Ted Hayter, from Newfoundland, sold books, toys, gifts, stationery, newspapers and sweets here during the war (1942) . Willie Turnbull, known as 'Willie Toot' delivered papers for them.

Wartime customers outside Macdonald's

Dorothy Macdonald,
Newsagent

Outside MacDonald's

M. & F. Hooper,
Newsagents, Confectioners, and Stationers

This building has a very recognisable pair of windows and separate single window on the other side of the door.

The shop was later owned by **Mr and Mrs Graham** (1972, 85) and then **Martin and Fiona Hooper** (1995) still operating as a ***News agent/Stationers***. Now no longer a shop, it houses the Highland Podiatry Services.

24 High Street
Milk from **Blairfoid Dairy** being delivered from a churn. Look closely to see the large jug in the milkman's hand which he used to measure out the milk for each delivery

Penneys had a ***fruit and vegetable*** shop here but this had gone by 1935. The Post Office was in a room in Hugh Penney's house but with its own door onto the High Street.

Penney, ***Greengrocer***

The Postmasters were **John Smith**, then **John Protheroe**. The Penney family continued to run the Post office (1985, 1995) until it moved into what had been Leslie Smith's Hardware Store at number 32.

24 High Street
The large front widow is useful evidence that this used to be a shop.

20 High Street

The Tea Room at the Cross

Alex Mackenzie Tea Rooms & Refreshment at the start of the century. It is not known what proclamation was being read out by the Provost.

Miller the Butcher

Bert Miller, *Butcher*
at the Market Cross

Meat was cut on great big wooden slabs. Only chickens were killed on site. He had a van which he used to travel around the outlying areas selling meat. There had always been a 'Miller the Butcher' in Fortrose. **Robert Miller** was a butcher in 1911 and was still there in the 1930s. He was followed by **Ian**, who wore a wig, then by his grandson Burt.

18 High St

Ona Matheson, *Draper*

This is the site of **Ona Matheson's *Drapers*** shop. Johanna Matheson had a draper's shop on the corner of Academy Street and High Street in the 1960s and 70s. Her shop was crammed full with men's, ladies, children's and baby clothes, knitting and sewing accessories and gifts. The Academy pupils went there to get kitted out in their school uniforms.

Eilean Dubh Restaurant

At the end of the 20th century it became the **'Tea Cosy'** run by the Comforts but is now the **Eilean Dubh Restaurant** and is a popular eating place for both visitors and local residents.

West End Stores, Canonbury Terrace (listed building)

'The Store ' was owned by **J & T Henderson.** Shopping in the first half of the 20th century was very different to today. Everything had to be weighed out on purchase so flour was sold by the boll, similarly oatmeal. A boll was about 140 pounds. Customers would make their own jams, picking fruit in season and buying 1cwt of sugar. They also sold 'millenium' flour, the finest oatmeal, sugars, dog cakes, poultry foods etc. etc.'.
Henderson's advertised themselves as Coal and General Merchants, House agents etc. as well as selling 'ironmongery, sporting ammunition, motor requisites and garage'.

J. & T. HENDERSON,
COAL & GENERAL MERCHANTS,
HOUSE AGENTS, &c.,
FORTROSE.

IRONMONGERY. SPORTING AMMUNITION.
MOTOR REQUISITES AND GARAGE.
MILLENIUM FLOUR —— FINEST OATMEAL —— SUGARS
DOG CAKES, POULTRY FOODS, &c., &c.

'The Store' was owned by the **Mackay** family from the mid 1950's until circa 1980. In addition to hardware and household goods in the shop, one could buy paraffin and agricultural supplies.

The West End Stores

Fortrose High Street from the Market Cross, 1912

Fortrose High Street from the Market Cross, 2012

Black Isle Grocery Counter

Pre-war Grocery Shop Interior, Beauly Museum

Retailing in Fortrose

General Trade and Craft Outlets 1825-2011 from Pigot's and Slater's Trade Directories (1825-1911), The North Star Guide to Fortrose and Rosemarkie (1930) and the Valuation Roll (1943,60,72, 85,95)

	1886	*1903*	*1911*	*1930*	*1943*	*1960*	*1972*	*1985*	*1995*	*2011*
Baker	2	2	2	2	2	2	2	1		2
Boot and Shoemaker	6	4			1	2	1			
Butcher	2	4	2	4	2	3	1	1	1	1
Chemist	1	1	1	1	1	1	1	1	1	1
Coal Merchant	1	1	1	1	1	1	1			
Cycle Agent		1	1		1					
Dairy				1	1	1				
Draper	4	5	3	3	3	3	2	2		
Dressmaker	5	2	2				1			
Fancy Goods		1	1	2	1	1	1	1	1	1
Garage			1	1	1	1	1	1	1	1
Greengrocer		1		2	1	1				

Grocer	**4**	**5**	**2**	**3**	**3**	**1**	**2**	**1**	**1**	**1**
Hairdresser			**1**	**1**	**1**	**2**	**2**	**2**	**1**	**1**
Ironmonger	**3**	**1**	**1**	**2**				**1**	**1**	
Post Office	**1**	**1**	**1**	**1**	**1**	**1**	**1**	**1**	**1**	**1**
Licensed Premises	**4**	**4**	**3**	**2**	**2**	**2**	**2**	**2**	**2**	**2**
Refreshment Rooms		**2**	**2**	**3**	**2**	**2**	**2**	**1**	**2**	**2**
Stationer	**1**	**1**		**2**	**1**	**1**	**1**	**1**	**1**	
Tailor	**4**	**3**	**5**	**1**	**1**					
Watchmaker	**2**	**2**	**4**	**2**		**1**				
Unspecified 'shops'					**2**	**1**	**1**	**3**	**2**	**1**

Chris and David Rendell
2013

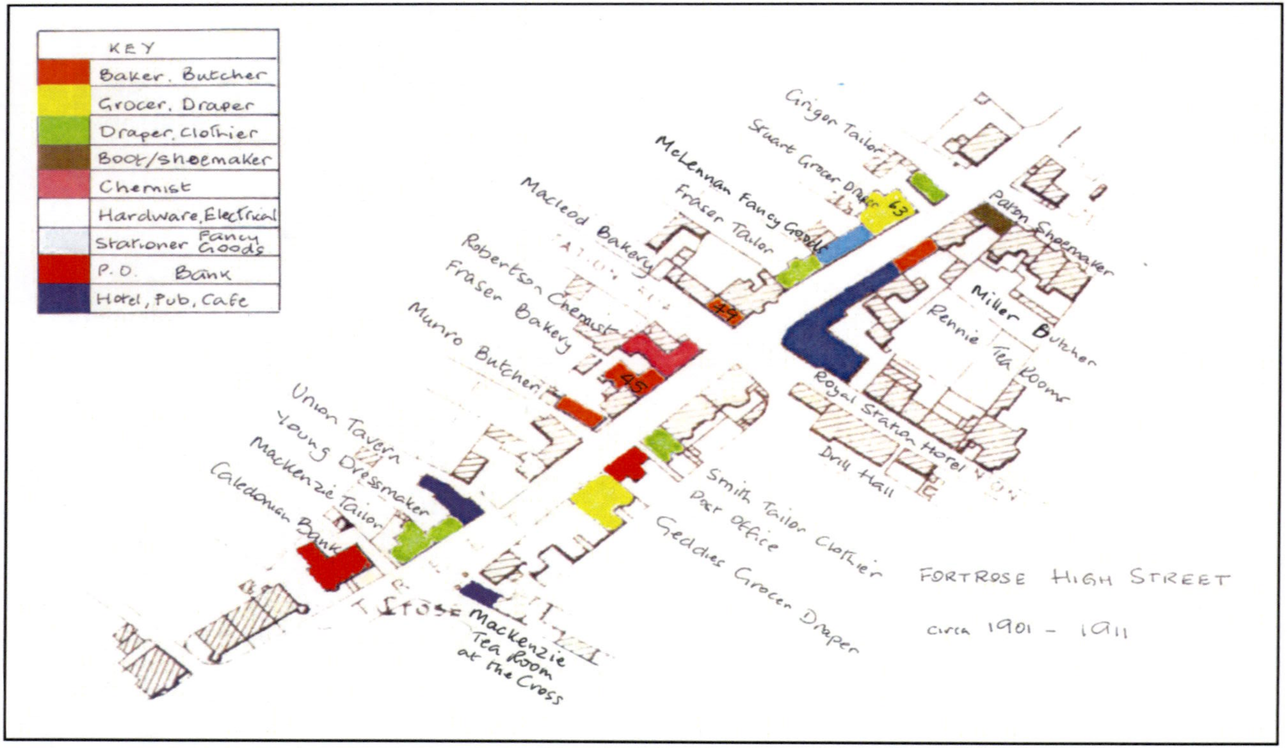

Fortrose High Street circa 1901-1911

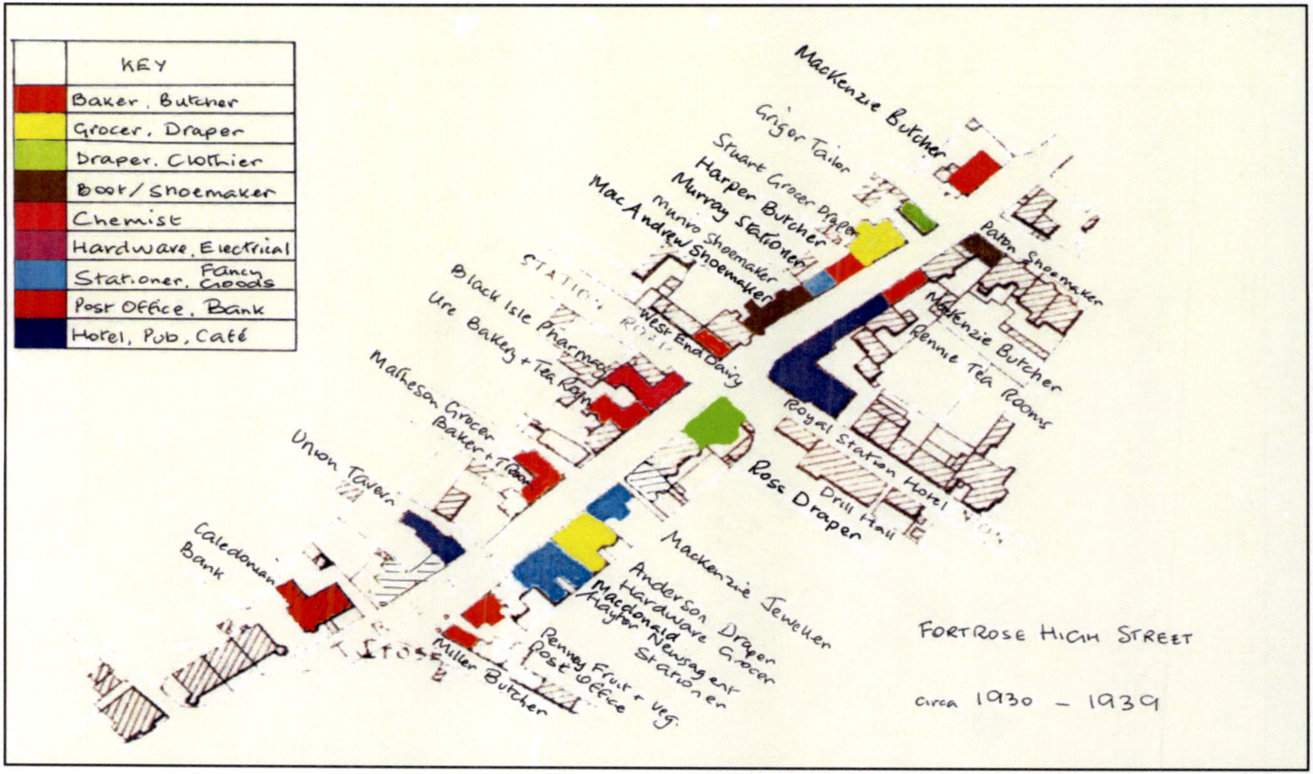

Fortrose High Street circa 1930-1939

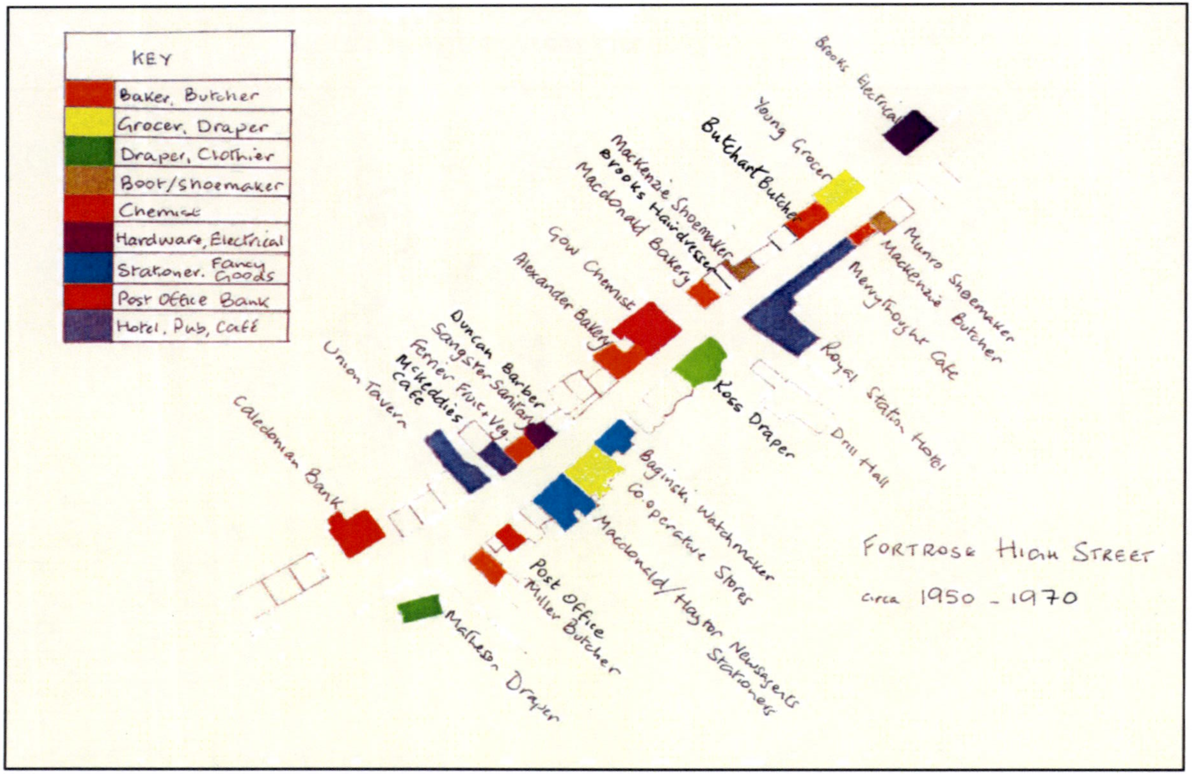

Fortrose High Street circa 1950-1970

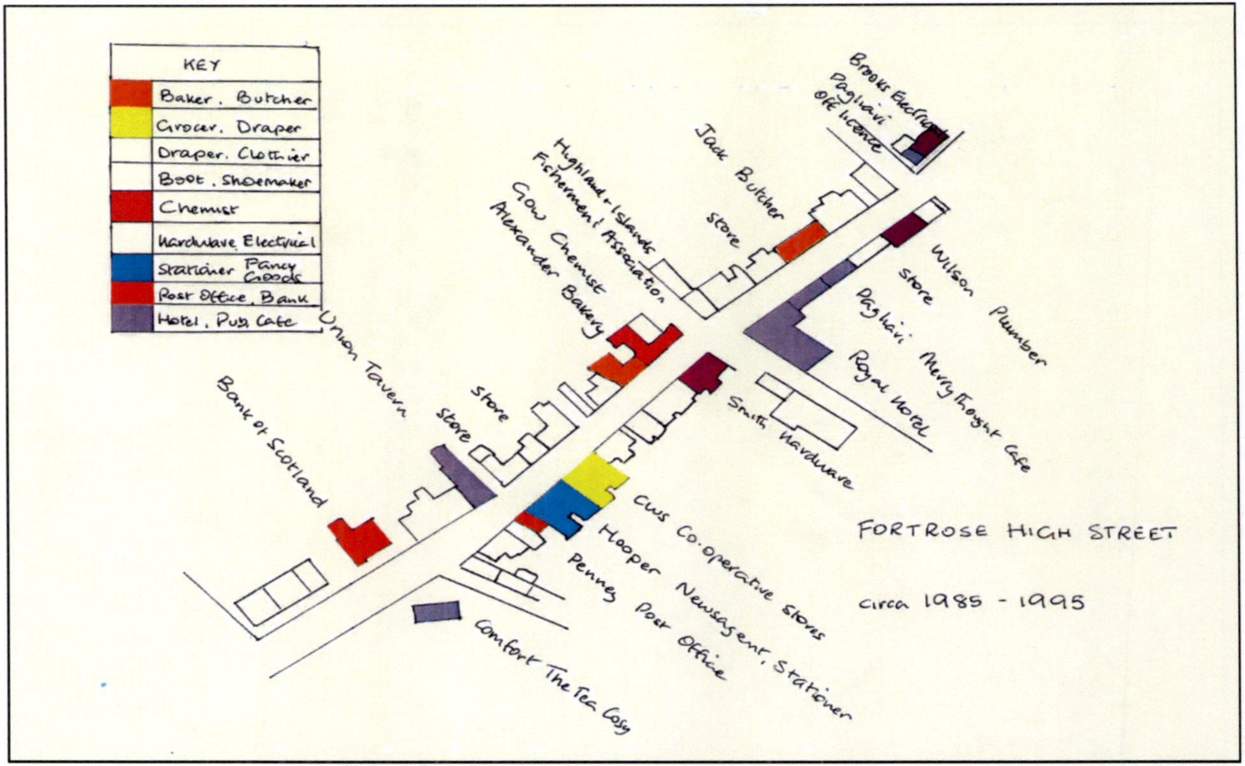

Fortrose High Street circa 1985-95

Fortrose High Street circa 2012

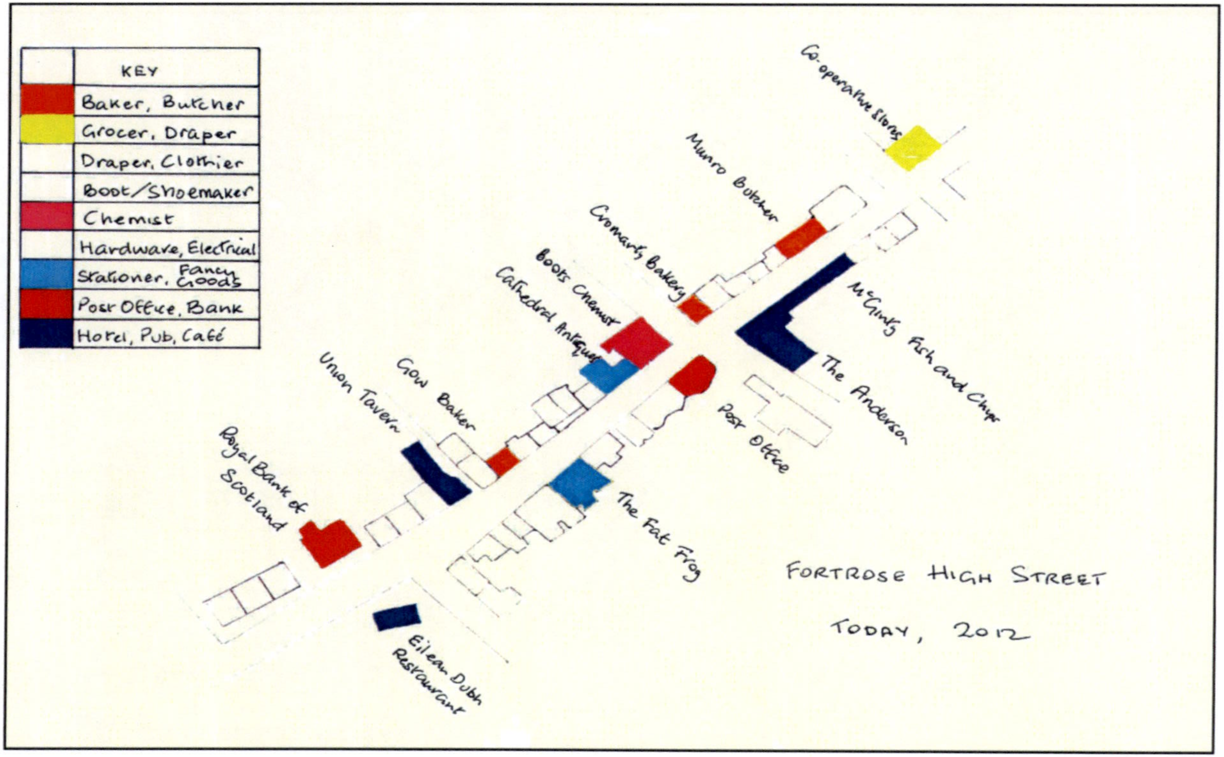

Rosemarkie

Rosemarkie High Street from the Market Cross, 1908

Rosemarkie High Street, 2013

Retailing in Rosemarkie

	1825 Pigot's	1901 Census	1911 Slater's	1930s North Star	1950s Third Stat Acc	1960 Val Roll	1985 Val Roll	2013 Survey
Baker		2	2	2		1	1	
Boot and Shoemaker	4	3	1	1	1			
Butcher		1	1	1	1	1	1	1
Blacksmith	1	2	1	1				
Cycle Agent								
Draper	1					1		
Dressmaker		2						
Fancy Goods		1	1					
Garage					1	1		
General Merchant				1				
Grocer	1	6	5	5	2	2		2

Horse Hirer			**1**					
Hairdresser								
Ironmonger			**1**	**2**	**1**			
Post Office		**1**	**1**	**1**	**1**	**1**	**1**	
Public House/Inn	**7**	**3**	**2**	**2**	**1**	**1**	**1**	**1**
Refreshment Rooms				**1**	**1**			**2**
Stationer		**1**		**1**				
Tailor	**3**	**1**	**1**	**1**		**1**		
Watchmaker								
Unspecified shops	**4**			**3**				**1**

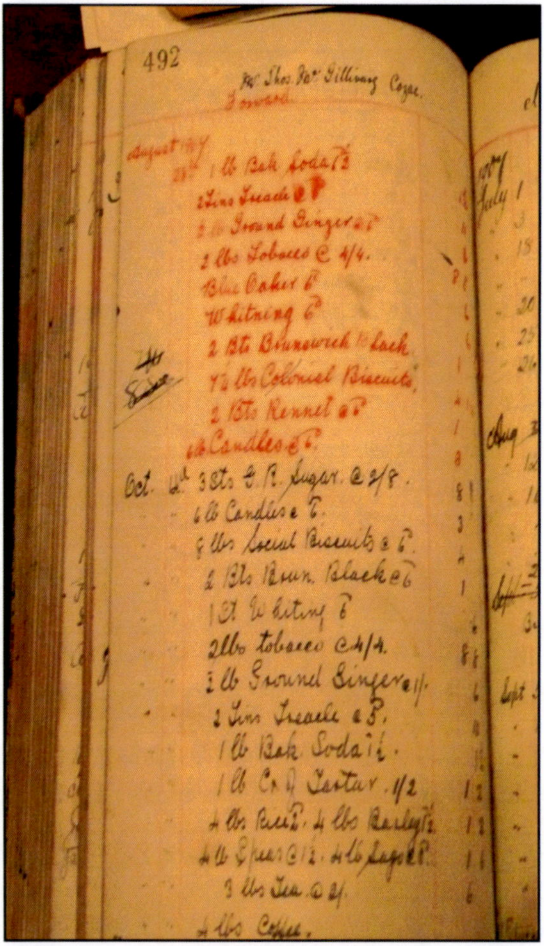

Grocery shop ledger

Housewives would make a list of what shopping they needed and in stable times could record how much they expected to pay for each item. Impulsive buying is a very recent trend associated with supermarket shopping.
The shop keeper would record all his sales in a ledger to monitor sales so that he could restock but also to prepare the monthly bill for those customers on account.

Rosemarkie High Street circa 1901-1911

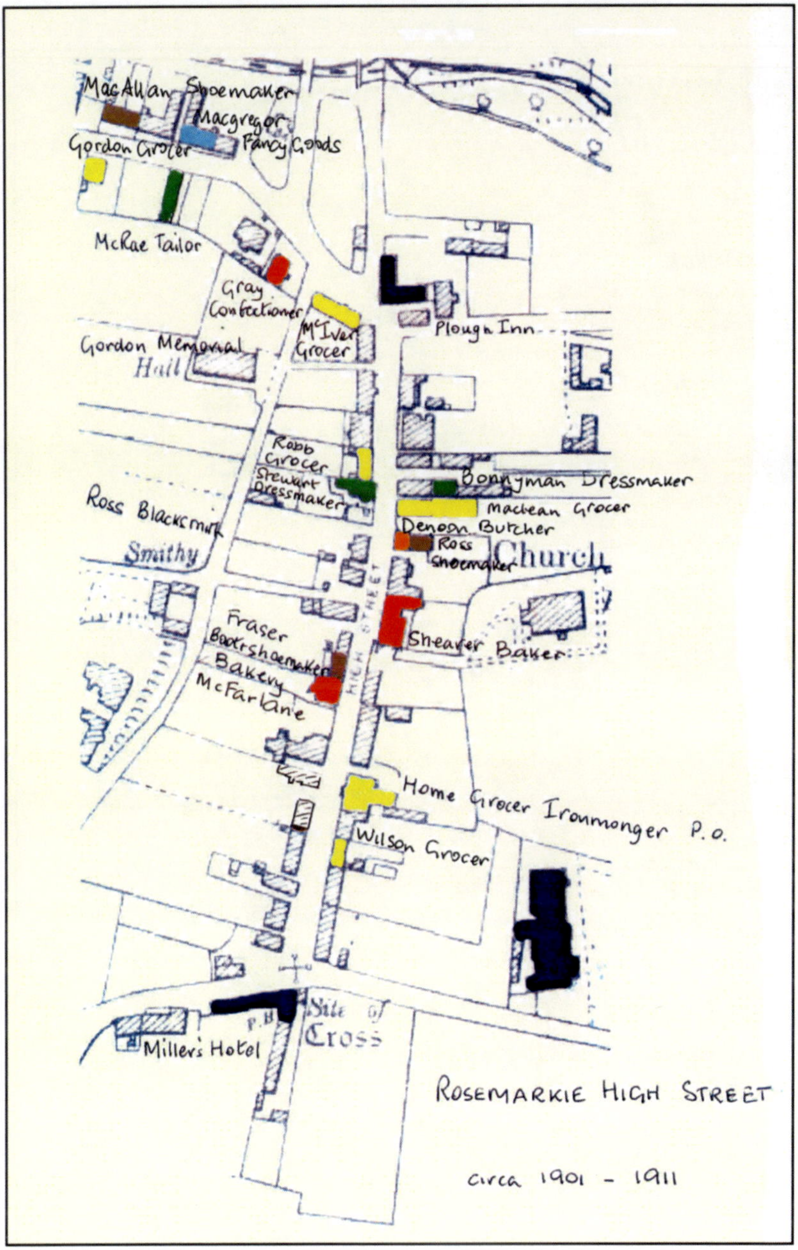

Rosemarkie High Street circa 1930-1939

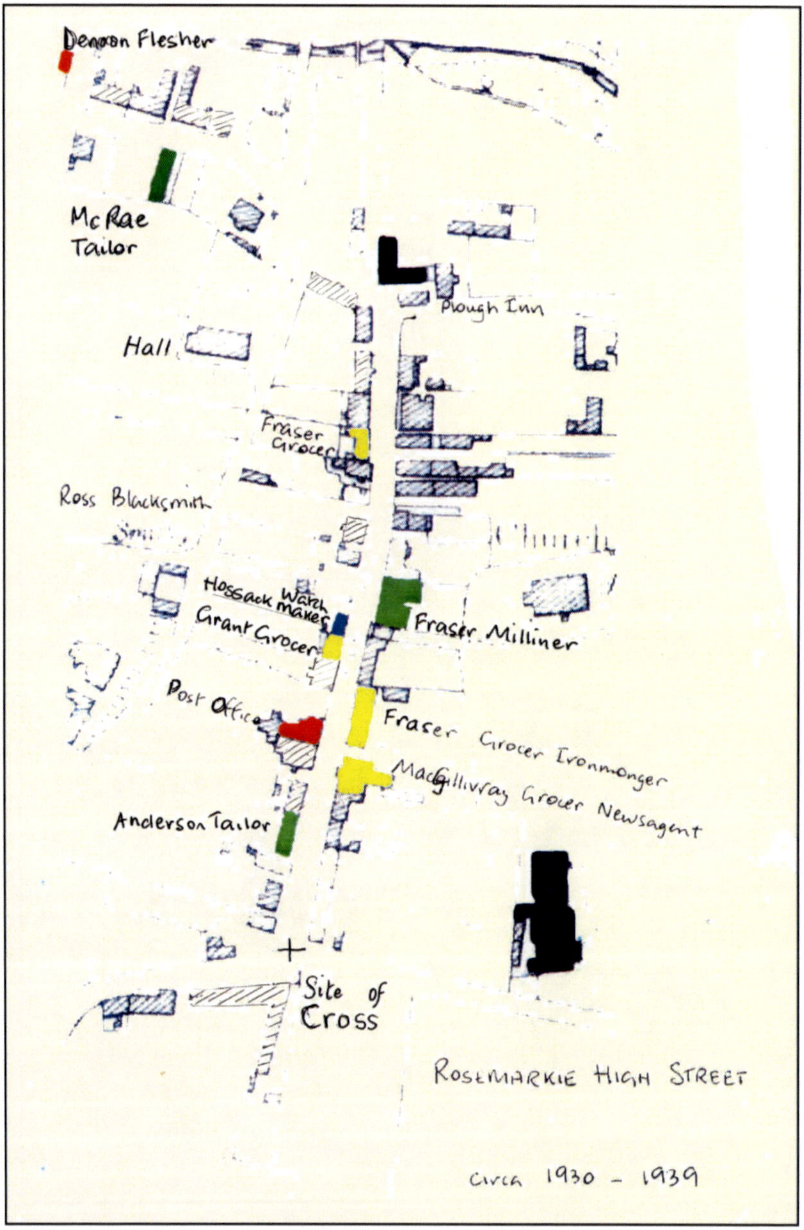

Rosemarkie High Street circa 1950-1970

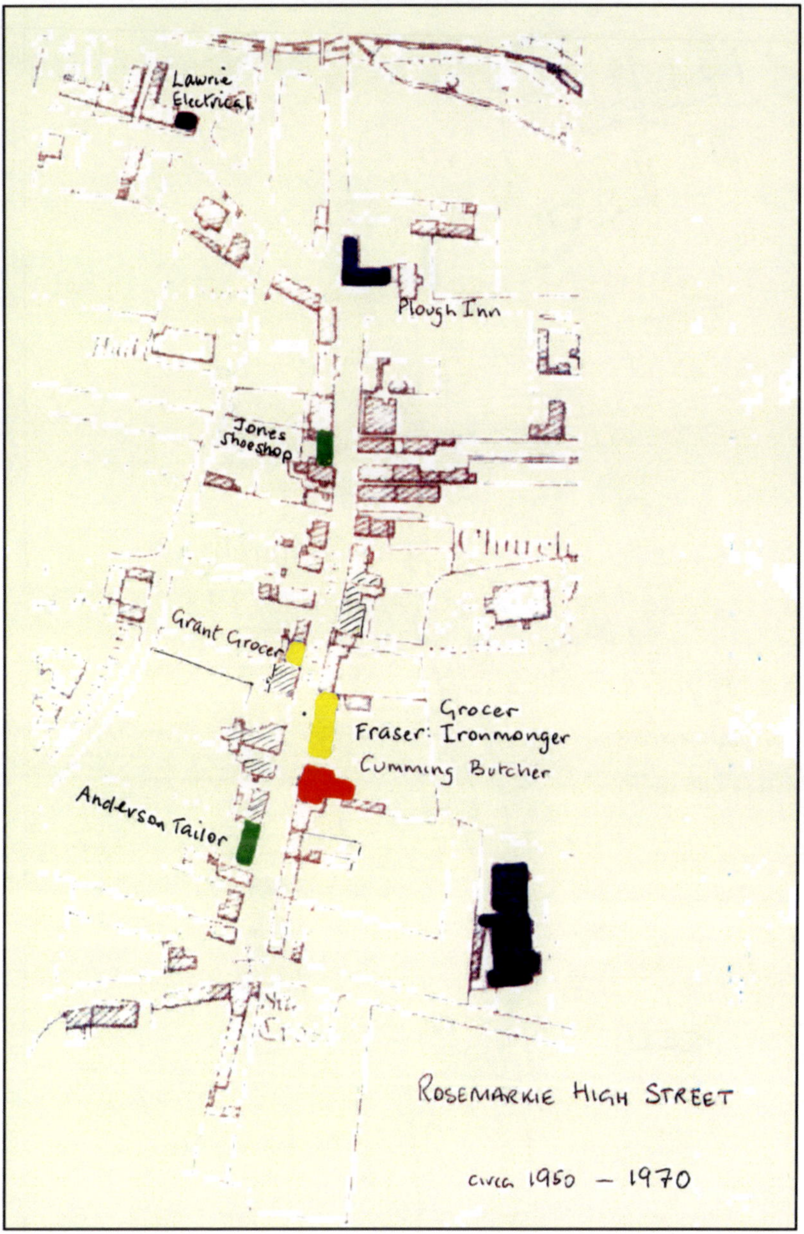

Rosemarkie High Street circa 1985-1995

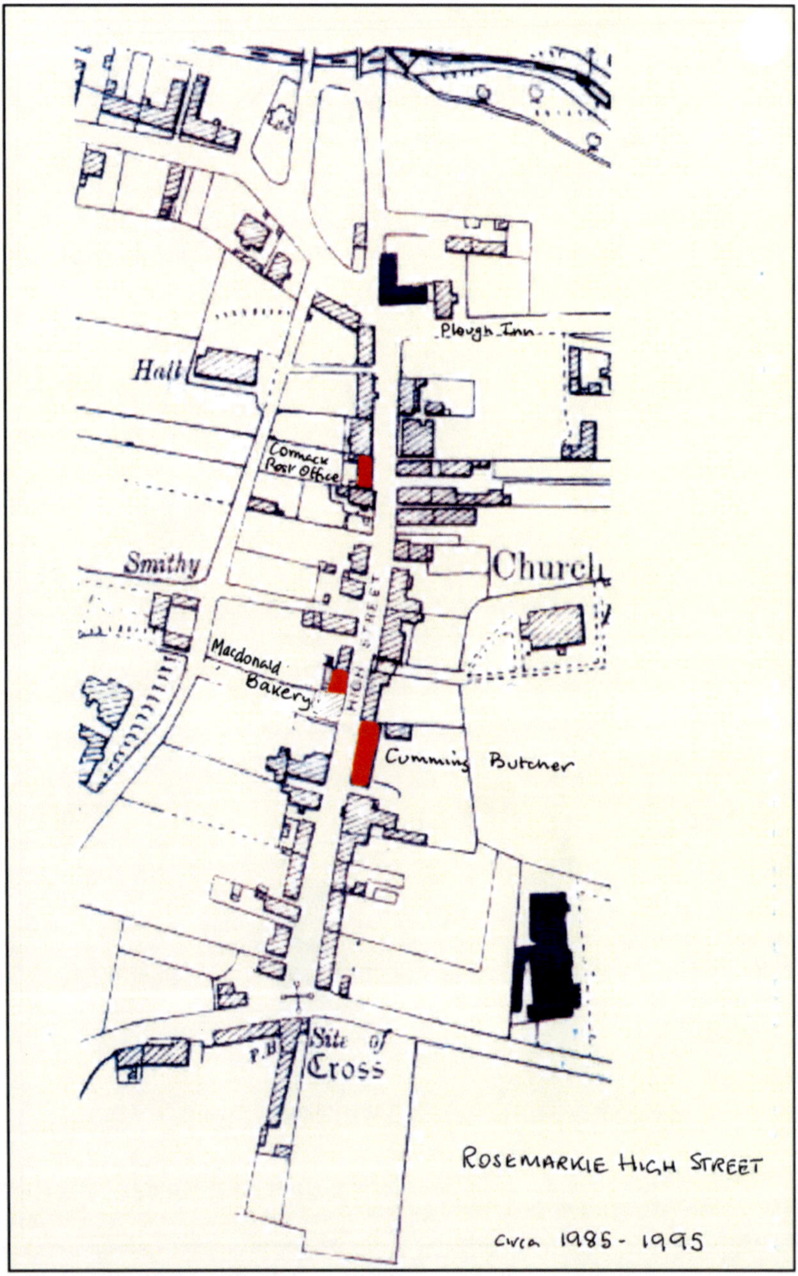

Rosemarkie High Street, 2013

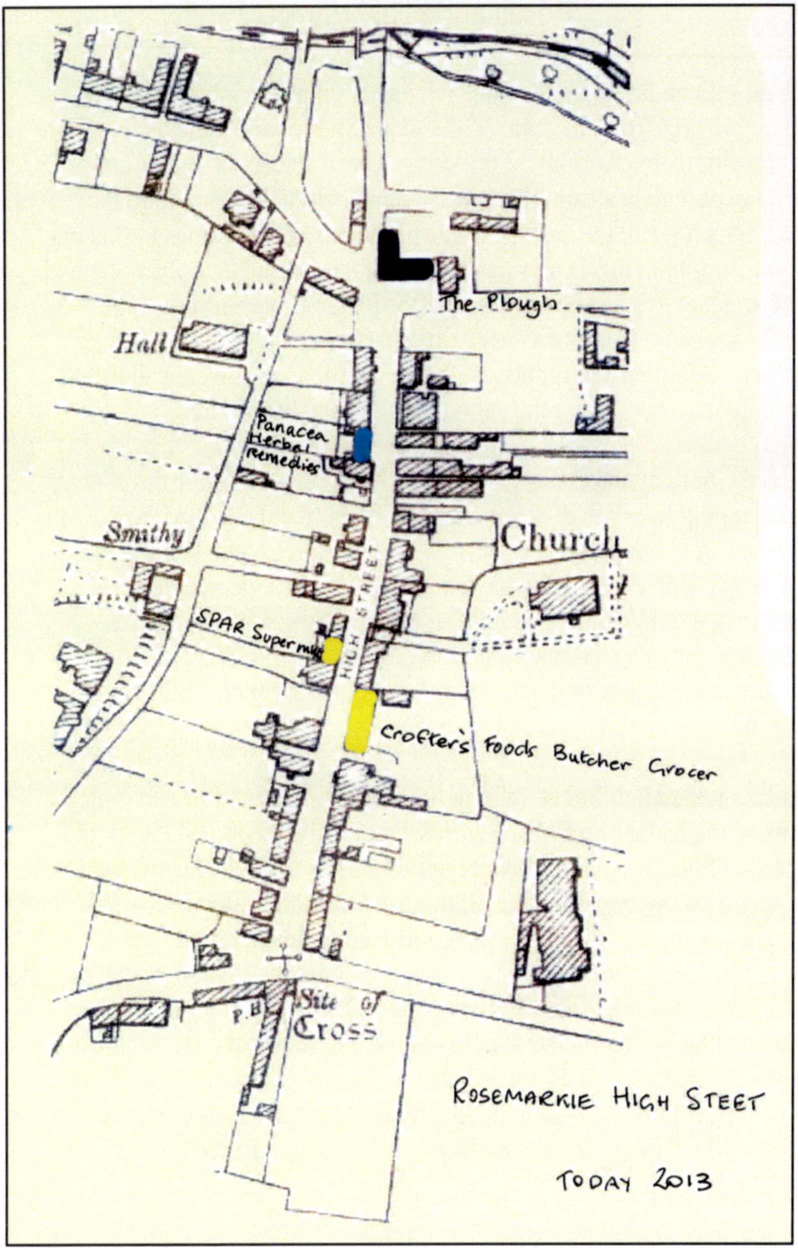

A Century of Shopping along Rosemarkie High Street

Rosemarkie today is a quiet, sleepy coastal village very popular with the holidaymakers from the caravan site who wander down the quaint High Street with its interesting old buildings. The impression of continuity with the past comes from the houses, many still gable-end on to the street which recall the ancient roods of the burgage holdings in this old Royal Burgh but this is an illusion for villages are always changing and evolving and this has been very true for Rosemarkie. Gone are the monks in the Pictish monastery. Taxed out of existence are the linen weavers with their retting ponds or 'the pows' as they were called and the salmon fishers along the shore have almost disappeared.

Even the holidaymakers have changed. Most now come for the caravan and camping rather than to stay in a big hotel like the Hawkhill, now the Marine Care Home. But the greatest changes have come about in the buildings themselves, some have decayed and disappeared, many altered or extended, while others have been completely rebuilt. Nevertheless there are many clues remaining as to a buildings' previous function. You will see the house with one big window or another with what looks like a shop front.

Exploring the High Street, talking to local residents and researching the Census, the Valuation Rolls, Slater's Trade Directories and the Inland Revenue Survey (1911), it has been possible to trace the history of a century of shopping along the High Street from the fifteen establishments in 1901 to the three remaining today.

In the first decade of the twentieth century there were four major shop-keepers who between them employed twelve shop assistants who lived in Rosemarkie as well as others from within the locality. The Big Four were Hugh Home, Grocer and Ironmonger, William Robb, Grocer, George Macfarlane, Baker and Kenneth MacRae, Master Tailor.

Some of their establishments continued as shops for half a century and one, William Robb's Grocers, is still a shop today at the bottom of the High Street, no longer a grocery meeting the daily needs of the local inhabitants but as 'Panacea' a visitor orientated establishment. Hugh Home's grocer/ironmongery occupied the most impressive building on Rosemarkie High Street . Both grocery shops were purpose built shop and house but the well-named 'Doric House', with its Greek style columns, has been a private residence since the 1960s.

Kenneth MacRae's tailoring business continued for over half a century and survived both Mr MacRae's death in the early 1930s and the destruction of his house/workshop by fire in the 1940s. The shortest lived shop belonged to George Macfarlane as he went out of business, bankrupt, in 1915.

Rosemarkie High Street at the beginning of the Twentieth Century

George Macfarlane, Baker

The old bakery at Tigh-an-Aigh

The Bakery – George McFarlane (Slater's Trade rectory,1911) had a house and shop with a bake house in the rear.

George McFarlane was a baker and confectioner employing his wife, Elizabeth, Donald Macdonald, journeyman baker and James H.F.Fraser, apprentice baker.

George McFarlane went bankrupt in 1915.

Local legend has it that James Fraser, the Baker in Fortrose, purchased the property to prevent it being run as a bakery in competition with him. Understandable perhaps as when George Macfarlane went bankrupt there were three bakers in the village as well as two bakeries in Fortrose.

James Fraser retired to Rosemarkie before the Second World War, to live in 'Seafield House'. When he sold up his Fortrose business he also sold his defunct Rosemarkie bakery to Harold Alexander, Baker in Fortrose. But again the bakehouse was never used as a bakery.

Miss Mary Ann MacGillivray took over as tenant in 1915 and renamed it **Tigh-an-Aigh**, She ran her general store in the premises opposite, 'Ivy Cottage' now called 'Doric House'.
Ice cream was sold in the summer months from 'Tigh-an-Aigh', the house that even now looks so much like a shop, but it continued to be a private residence.

Freda Bassindale, Rosemarkie People and Places, describes how the bricks from the oven have been used to create a paved area at the back of the house.

M. MACGILLIVRAY,

HIGH-CLASS GROCER : : :
NEWSAGENT AND STATIONER,

THE STORES, ROSEMARKIE.

Golf, Tennis, and Bathing Requisites Stocked.

Mary Ann MacGillivray's advert in the North Star (1930)

37 High Street

Panacea, Herbal Remedies which sells tourist type items like rocks, gems, and aromatherapy.
Panacea, Herbal Remedies removed from Dingwall in 2011.

The interior of Panacea
The original boarding and shelves date from when it was a grocery shop.

In 1911 the shop was a ***Cash Grocers*** run by **William Robb**. Note the 'cash' grocer banner, this was not a high class establishment like Hugh Home's Grocery which served the middle class customers paying 'on account'.

Robb, *Grocer*

In the 1930s Rosemarkie boasted a high-class ironmongery, grocery and provisions, D.& G. Fraser. **Daniel Fraser** rented the shop at 37 High Street according to the Valuation Rolls for 1931- 39 and 1942. Daniel specialised in ***grocery and provisions***. He set up his brother George who had been gassed in the Great War, as ***ironmonger*** 'up the street' at number 18 High Street.

Daniel Fraser

Later, it became **Jones, the shoe shop**.

Catherine Macpherson Cormack Jones sold everything one could possibly need in the drapery line (Val Roll 1946,55-65,85).

Mrs Jones had a mobile van and was still selling shoes, drapery and haberdashery around the Black Isle in the 1970s. Sandra Jack described going into the shop as ***'entering Aladdin's cave'***.

'Ivy House', renamed 'Doric House'

Hugh Home, *Grocer and Ironmonger*

This imposing classical building with its pillars and steps up to the door was built by Andrew Steavenson, a General Merchant. Steavenson was Provost of Fortrose in 1837. John Carpenter Steavenson, General Merchant sold rifles, furniture and watches and leased salmon fishing from Mr Hogarth who had bought 'Drummarkie'. Hogarth changed the name 'Drummarkie' to 'St Helena' when he planted willow cuttings from Napoleon's grave there. It has reverted to its original name but the willow tree is believed to be still there.

Hugh Home had his ***Grocer, Ironmonger*** business there. His son **Michael** ran the ***Post Office*** according to Slater's Trade Directory 1911 and the 1911 Census.

At the beginning of the twentieth century, service was everything and Hugh Home employed several assistants. Although the hours were long, over seventy hours per week and the wages low, working in a shop was seen as better than going into domestic service.

There would be a variety of tasks to be done as well as serving the customer for grocery supplies came in large amounts by the barrel and had to be hand packed for the individual customer. The 'boy' would then deliver the goods purchased on his bike.

When Hugh retired in1913 it was occupied by **Mary Ann MacGillivray**, a ***'High Class' Grocer, Newsagent and Stationer***. 'The Stores' also sold golf, tennis and bathing requisites. Rosemarkie was a popular holiday location at this time. Mary Ann's establishment also kept very long hours and was known to stay open, on occasion, to midnight.

The Shop Act of 1912 attempted to limit the numbers of hours worked by shop assistants by instigating half day closing but could not prevail over enthusiastic owners. The delivery 'boy' then was Jimmy Lumsden. Mary Ann MacGillivray retired in 1944.

'Doric House' today

The Scottish Co-operative Society *Grocery and Drapery* took over 'Doric House' for about ten years. The SCWS had been established in 1867 and by 1900 one in ten Scots were members and shareholders but it did not reach the Black Isle until the Second World War.

There was usually a grocery and provisions, drapery, a butchery or fleshing and a bakery.

1960 **Kenneth Cumming** had his **butchery** there before moving next door to what is now 'Crofters Foods'.

3 High Street

home of Rod Anderson, *Tailor*

Rod Anderson who was employed by Mrs Margaret MacRae (widow of Kenneth MacRae, *Master Tailor*) built a shed in his back garden so that he could continue working after the War Department, World War Two, requisitioned the MacRae's former home of Craigview. In 1944 Polish soldiers accidentally burnt down the house in Bridge Street and it was always afterwards called the 'burnt house'.

The property Rod Anderson rented, 3 High Street, was classed as uninhabitable by 1955 and his shed valued at only £2.
He was still working as a tailor there, however in 1960.

There are several tailors, drapers and dressmakers recorded in the 1901 Census for although most people made their own clothing, men might own one tailored suit for best and women would use a dressmaker for special outfits. The Census shows **William Young** (18) draper's apprentice and **Daniel Fraser** (24) tailor, boarding with a washerwoman, Isabella Corbett, at this address.

In 1911 there were nine clothiers in the village. The villagers at the beginning of the 20th century would have been astounded at the number of clothes people own nowadays. They were familiar with natural materials, linen, cotton or wool. Nylon began to be available just before the Second World War but the wide range of man made materials available now did not come in until the late 1950s. However Master Tailor Kenneth Macrae who employed 4 tailors, would probably not have been very impressed with the quality of modern clothing in our throw away society.

Kenneth MacRae, ***Master Tailor***

The other tailors, particularly the ladies dressmakers and seamstresses 'worked from home on their own account'. **Margaret Stewart** and **Barbara Bonnyman** as dressmakers were a cut above **Isabella Clark** and **Janet Ross** who could only sew seams.

There were also several other individuals, both men and women, who worked from home on their own account. These were **Alexander Fraser**, ***Boot and shoemaker*****, Alexander MacAllan,** ***Shoemaker*** in Bridge Street and **Thomas Ross,** ***Shoemaker***.

The Ross family rented a half house, shop and garden (Val Roll 1909) to **John Denoon,** ***Flesher*****,** (famed as the last surviving Rosemarkie Veteran of the 1st Inverness Volunteers who attended Queen Victoria's 'Wet Review' when he died in 1942).
John Denoon lived in a cottage round the corner in Bridge Street. By 1911 the Ross family were renting part of their property to **Robert Miller,** ***Butcher*** (Val Roll 1911/12). Miller had his fleshings at 42 High Street, Fortrose.

The Ross home is described as an 'old thatched' cottage' next door to Groam House, now the museum. Thomas Ross is recorded as shoemaker in both the 1901 and the 1911 Census. He was still working aged 78 in 1911. His wife Margaret (70) had had 12 children but 10 died. Their surviving son, William, was a mason's labourer.

The hand- made shoes were called 'Black Isle Boxies' they were so shapeless. This meant that they could be changed from foot to foot to even the wear. Boot and shoe making was revolutionised by the invention of the sewing machine in 1846. By the end of the nineteenth century the mass manufacture of boots and shoes threatened the livelihood of individual boot and master shoe makers but there was still a steady demand for shoe repair. Boots and shoes would have the sole and/or the heel replaced several times.

Christine McIver, ***Grocer*** ran her small shop from a room in the family home. **Catherine Wilson** (79) was a ***Grocer shopkeeper*** at her home with the help of her granddaughter Catherine Home (24). **John Gordon**, ***Grocer*** had bigger premises as his property is described as a shop and house and he was an employer employing his niece Lizzie Miller (23) as shop assistant.

In the same way **Jamesina 'Minnie' Gray** worked as a ***Confectioner*** from her Aunt Madalina Arthur's home in the High Street and **Jeannie Shearer** is described as a '***Baker's shopkeeper'*** working from her home in Church Place in the 1901 Census.

It has not been possible to locate these shops precisely except where there is a good description like **Miss Lizzie Macgegor, *Fancy Goods and Stationery*** which was reported to be a stone house, slated and appearing to have attic rooms, according to the Inland Revenue Survey (1911). This has been identified as the newsagents in the left-hand part of Albion Cottages, Bridge Street.

Named premises are much easier although names are often changed with new owners. **Annie Douglas McLean, *Grocer*** ran her drapery, millinery and stationery business from Groam House now the Groam House Museum.

Groam House Museum

The unusual name 'Groam' was chosen by Mr Mclean, a Merchant, when he removed from Groam, Kirkhill.

Miller's Hotel

Miller's Hotel at the top of the High Street was run in 1911, by **Miss Margaret Miller**, S***pirit Dealer*** and was owned by Margaret and her brother John who lived in Rose Cottage.

Miller's Hotel

Elizabeth Sutherland, the local historian and author, writes that Miller's Hotel was a coaching inn with four horses, wagonettes and a phaeton.

The New Year's Day 'Bools' game used to start at Miller's Hotel with men from two teams hurling a small iron ball down to the Ness then back to the public house for a celebration drink.

The Plough Inn

A long established public house, extensively renovated by **John Robb** in 1907, Robb was still the publican in Slater's Trade Directory, 1911. John Robb bought the disused meal mill, 'Ootseys', at the bottom of Mill Road and turned it into a Laundry. The Laundry would wash bedding for the army based at Fort George. Robb employed 26 workers, 20 of them women.

The bedclothes were transported to and fro by ferry from Ardesier to Chanonry Point. Several carters were employed to collect laundry from Cromarty, Invergordon and Inverness as well as Fort George. It is said that although the sheets were put round the mill wheel and wetted the blankets just got a good shake before being returned as 'clean'. Sheets and blankets were spread out on the grass along the sea front from the mill right down to the Chanonry lighthouse.

The Plough Inn

The Plough Inn continues to be a public house and also serves good quality food in competition with the 'Crofters', a bistro type restaurant in what used to part of The Hawkhill Hotel and there is also the 'Beach Café' at the mouth of the Fairy Glen, which sells ice cream and sandwiches.

An advert for the Plough Inn from the North Star(1930)

PLOUGH INN, ROSEMARKIE

ESTABLISHED 1690.

A REAL HIGHLAND FAVOURITE.

Visitors should see Genuine Relics of Auld Scotland.

REFRESHMENTS AS SCOTLAND ONLY CAN PRODUCE.

Real Scotch Liqueurs, Ales, Brandies, Spirits, Wines, &c.
The Best only Stocked.

GARAGE AND STANCE.

R. McKENZIE, *Proprietor.*

Back Road

Alexander Ross, *Blacksmith*

Recorded in Slater's 1911 and marked on the OS map 1904 edition as 'Smithy' next to the junction on Courthill Road. Jenny Paterson can remember a smithy there when she was a child in the 1930s. Alexander Ross owned both the smithy and the adjacent cottage. He employed William Alexander as a journeyman blacksmith. He rented several rigs of land in the locality. His son Alexander was joint tenant in 1931/2 but Alexander Ross died in 1936, aged 71 and by 1938/9 the smithy is recorded as 'empty'. The buildings both house and smithy are described as 'old', constructed from stone with a slate roof (IRS 1911).

The blacksmith was an important man in the village for he would manufacture many iron items for use on the farm or at home as well as shoe horses.

Kenneth Jack took over as village blacksmith in the late 1930s.
He is recorded at 2 Bridge Street 1938/9.

Bridge Street Cottages

Folk memories can persist for a long time. The first 'shops' evolved from the medieval market stalls and began to replace the twice-yearly fairs allowed by Royal Charter. Although the market was last held in the early 1800s, villagers in Rosemarkie still remember its location 'up the Brae Cross'. The Fortrose St Boniface Fair with its festival atmosphere, survives to the present day.

Several locals mentioned a 'glover' working from home and selling gloves at the market or bringing gloves to the Cross to be sent further afield. At first it seemed that this might be **Miss Mary Mackenzie**, Cloy Cottage, who is recorded in the 1901 Census as a **'ladies maid'** since she would have had the appropriate fashion knowledge. But the 1911 Census records her as working as a nurse so this seems unlikely. A man called Davidson worked as a Glover from Lilac Cottage in 1760. The First Statistical Account, 1791 records two glovers in Rosemarkie parish.

There are no recent records of 'glovers' in the village.

Lilac Cottage

In 1930 the North Star published a booklet promoting Fortrose and Rosemarkie as holiday destinations with a series of adverts including this one.

Nobody seems to recall Watson's the Butcher who advertised 'pickled meat' a speciality, but a Robert Watson of Rosemarkie was declared bankrupt in 1945.

One business whose location at a certain date can be relied upon, is the Post Office. The 1904 edition of the Ordnance Survey map for Rosemarkie records its position on the High Street. Not requiring any large specialist equipment like a bakery or smiddy means that the Post office can be quite mobile and need not stay in one set location.

1904	Post Office, 9 High Street.
1911	Post Master Michael Home, 12 High Street.
1920's	Post Office between Plough Inn and Seafield
	Post Mistress Jane or Jeannie .Macandrew
1931-36	P M Jeannie Macandrew, 20 High Street.
Late 1930s	Post Mistress, Mabel Fraser, 9 High Street.
Post 1945	Post Master, Daniel Fraser, 18 High Street.
1971	Post Master, Alexander Alexander, 18 High St
1985	Post Master Cormack, 37 High Street.
1995	Post Master Straw, 37 High Street.
2001	Post Master Peter McLoughlin, 37 High Street.
2005	Post Office closed.

Post Master Straw had the terrifying experience of being robbed at knife-point by two drug addicts from Alness.

The Post Office

9 High Street or 'Limetree' was the Fraser family home.

George and Mabel Fraser lived here with his mother Jessie and his brother Daniel. The brothers were business partners in:

D.& G. Fraser
Ironmonger/Grocery
and Post Office.

In the Highlands, isolated communities could only survive by being virtually self-sufficient. Markets were far apart and transport, except by sea, difficult. Progress in the form of manufactured goods, pre-packaged items, chain shops and self service supermarkets came late to this area.

Shops that sell a bit of everything persist even into the twenty- first century on the Black Isle. In Rosemarkie this one-stop-shop role was played by the Fraser brothers. **Daniel and George Fraser** described their business as a high class ironmongery, grocery and general merchants selling a variety of provisions.

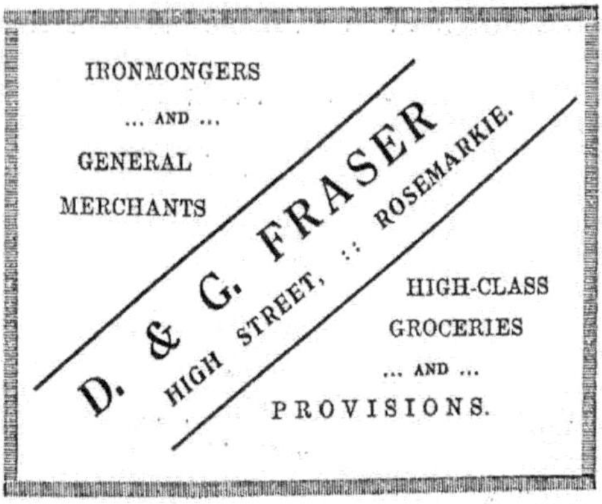

Daniel concentrated on grocery and provisions at 37 High Street until he moved up the street in place of his late brother George at number18 High Street.

George had been a baker's apprentice but having been gassed in the First World War his health was not good enough to sustain the physical demands of bakery so he ran the ironmongery section in the family shop.

After his brother's early death, at the age of 47, in 1938, Daniel managed both parts of the business for a time. He closed his shop at 37 High Street in the mid 1940's and moved his sister-in-law Mabel's Post Office business into the grocery to complement the range of services provided at 18 High Street.

Daniel Fraser was still running the grocery/ironmongers at 18 High Street in 1955.

No one can recall when Daniel closed his business but the shop at number 18 stood empty for some years in the mid 1960's.
The shop was re-established by **Alexander Alexander**, the Fortrose baker, in the early 1970's. He kept the Post Office and added fresh bread to the grocery section. Then **Kenneth Cumming, *Butcher*** moved in from 'Doric House' next door for many years until 2009 (Val Roll 1985, 95) .

Rosemarkie came close to losing its butcher's shop when Kenneth Cumming closed and although various individuals took over they were unable to make a profitable return until Richard Comfort expanded it into a first class 'Deli' specialising in haggis, sausages, pies and ready made meals to unique recipes. It has very recently been taken over by Penelope Keith's husband and the shop is managed by their son.

Crofters Foods with its excellent range of goods is once again providing Rosemarkie with a one-stop fresh food shop selling meat, vegetables, and bakery goods.

Crofters Foods

After the First World War the number of shops in Rosemarkie shrank to only six. In the first half of the twentieth century there were to be tremendous developments in the way we shop. Gone were the small shops in private homes and many, in towns, to replaced by purpose built shops and shopping arcades.

Nineteenth century industrialisation generated a new type of High Street. Mass produced tinned goods changed the emphasis on what we bought and ate. Shoppers began to demand goods with brand names like 'Bird's' Custard or 'Keiller' Marmalade and 'Hovis' Bread.

The drop in demand for home baking and cooking curtailed the entrepreneurial opportunities for families to make some extra money from their garden produce. Times were hard. By 1930 there were 3 ruinous buildings, 2 uninhabitable as well as a further 2 unoccupied of the High Street, nearly a fifth of the 40 or so buildings on Rosemarkie's High Street were lying empty!

The shops that survived were D & G Fraser's Ironmongery and Grocery, Mary Ann MacGillivray's General Store with its emphasis on the holiday trade, the Post Office and the butcher. Kenneth Macrae continued his tailoring business in Bridge Street.

Fraser, *Milliner*

A new shop came to Rosemarkie in the 1930s with first **Margaret Fraser** (Val Roll 1931/2) and then **Christina Fraser** (Val Roll 1935/6,38/9) ***making and selling hats*** from 26 High Street.

At that time all ladies wore hats so a milliners was a useful addition to the range of village shops. Nevertheless the improved transport network meant that ladies could also travel into Inverness to shop by either bus and ferry or train from Fortrose.

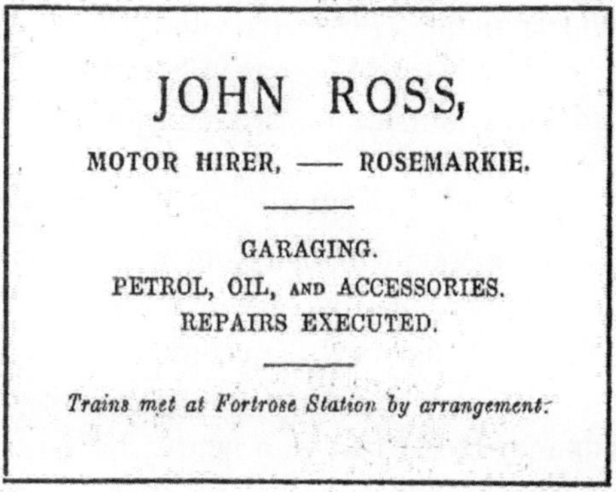

Fortrose station opened in 1894 with a branch line to Muir of Ord where it joined the main track to Dingwall and the North or Inverness and south on to Edinburgh.

The establishment of a comprehensive rural bus network by the 1930s made it possible to travel by bus to Cromarty or Inverness and back in one day. This encouraged the village shopper to try out alternative shopping opportunities for a range of everyday goods as well as specialist items.

By 1950 there were only four shops along Rosemarkie High Street. There were two grocers still, Daniel Fraser, Grocery and Ironmongery at 18 High Street and Lewis Grant opposite at number 17. Kenneth Cumming, Butcher at 14 High Street and Catherine Jones, shoes, drapery and haberdashery at 37 High Street. Rod Anderson was still working from home as a tailor.

Lewis Grant ran a traditional ***Grocery***, buying in fresh rabbit meat from schoolboy, Mark Grigor, who caught the rabbits on his father's farm before going onto school. It was a bright cheerful shop with a modern extension but it was proving ever more difficult for village shops to meet their customers needs. Grant's had modernised by delivering their customer's groceries by van rather than by bicycle.

The increased ownership of the motorcar would have a powerful influence on where we live and work as well as where we shop. Owning a car made living in a village like Rosemarkie an attractive proposition again, slowing the move away from the village as the number of agricultural jobs declined with the mechanisation of farming. New houses began to appear on the edges of the village towards the end of the century. Similar new-builds began in Fortrose and the local population increased, and continues to increase, with more new estates planned.

The changing nature of the village population with more and more people travelling to work and shop in town since the opening of the Kessock Bridge in 1982, means that while the local shop continues to be essential for those without transport, like the elderly, for the majority of the inhabitants, the village shop may be used only for items which have been 'forgotten' in the main weekly shop at the supermarket.

By 1985 Grant's premises had been taken over by **Macdonald's of Avoch, Bakery**. The shop was not just an outlet for the bakery but continued to sell a range of grocery goods using the services of the **SPAR** voluntary wholesaling group. These wholesaling groups help promote recognised brands and give the independent grocer the benefits of better purchasing power as well as allowing participation in regional and national marketing initiatives.

In Rosemarkie it was this grocery shop that was to take the next big step towards modernisation. In 1993 the new owners, Mr and Mrs Phillips, who still live in the village, introduced 'self- service'. When Mr and Mrs Phillips bought the SPAR they were anxious to preserve as much as possible of the original shop while at the same time bringing it up to date. Inside the shop the wooden cladding on the walls and the wooden shelves remained but the counter across the middle had to go to allow for self-service.

The SPAR Supermarket, formerly Grant's Grocery and Macdonald's Bakery

When the Grants lived above the shop, customers were accustomed to knock on the door for service if the shop was shut. As the Phillips lived several doors away this was not convenient but to maintain the level of service Mr Phillips would open up on Christmas morning while Mrs Phillips was at home cooking Christmas dinner. That two hour period had the highest footfall of the year as Mr Phillips was kept busy supplying the batteries needed for the new toys the children were desperate to play with.

The change to self-service reflects the faster pace of life and the rise of individual independence. Modern shoppers are in a hurry. Time is seen as a scarce resource when doing essential shopping. They do not want to queue and be given the items requested. There had been several Acts of Parliament to try to regulate and protect customers through standardised weights and measures and so give them a fair measure of unadulterated goods but customers prefer the freedom to browse and to choose their own apples or pears without intervention from the shopkeeper.

One big advantage of the pre-packaged self service item was the price label. When prices were stable and housewives knew to a farthing how much their shopping would cost, they might trust the local shopkeeper who would not have had any prices showing. Haggling or 'higgling' over the price was common. Customers in rural areas continued to barter into the 20th century. But in times of rapid inflation, totalling the amount to be paid before reaching the till, saved the customer from potential embarrassment.

The individual, independent retailer in the village High Street is struggling to compete with the chain stores in an increasingly uneven battle. By 2006, independent grocers could claim less than 3% of the grocery trade.

In the 1950s and 60s Rosemarkie had had its own electrical store, **Andrew Lawrie, *Electrics*** on the corner of Bridge Street, now a private residence.

Andrew Lawrie's white goods and electronics evolved from the traditional hardware shop but required an expensive range of stock. There has been such great competition for white goods that even national chain stores like 'Comet' have gone to the wall.

Andrew Lawrie, *Electrics*

Not only has the number and range of shops declined but villages are no longer self-sufficient in the services provided. Workshops, which were an extension of a master craftsman's home, have disappeared. Rosemarkie has lost its blacksmith, tailor, dressmaker, shoemaker, milliner, miller, carpenter and plumber.

Some new services emerged over the century like carter/carrier and garage but these too struggle to compete with the national chains. Petrol or diesel is always more expensive at the nearest local garage like that at Tore, than it is at Tesco or Morrisons and the garage that used to be in Bridge Street is long gone.

The decline in self-sufficiency in the village means villagers can no longer rely upon their neighbours to supplement their family skills and garden produce. They themselves are no longer vital to the social network which knits a community together. Rosemarkie has endeavoured to replace this community interdependence with community activities based around the Gordon Memorial Hall like the SWRI and special exhibitions like that celebrating the linen weaving which had been Rosemarkie's main industry in the eighteenth century.

The modern shopkeeper understands the need to offer specialist services and produce to attract customers. The three shops surviving in Rosemarkie today are the SPAR, self-service supermarket; the Crofters' Deli with its unique, high quality fresh produce and Panacea the Herbal Remedy establishment which is much more than just a shop selling herbs as it offers a range of meditational services like Reiki, a hands on form of alternative medicine. There is also a shop hidden in the Groam House Museum, selling a wide range of books, cards, jewellery and holiday souvenirs.

Shopping has become a favourite leisure activity for many, even a social 'ritual'. Shoppers flock to the giant shopping malls, which provide all-inclusive 'entertainment' when shopping for specific items like clothing or electronics. The number and range of out of town retail outlets continue to grow at the expense of the traditional High Street. Shopping is now such a 'fun' activity that people expect to enjoy shopping even when on a camping holiday at the seaside so the Groam House Museum shop, Panacea, the Plough Bistro and The Crofters restaurant all add to Rosemarkie's attractiveness as a holiday destination.

The First World War has been recognised as a watershed in the history of shopping. Never again would Rosemarkie or Fortrose have so many retail outlets/workshops. The changing nature of shopping with its emphasis on mass-produced brand names plus the improvements to the transport network has led to a steady decline in High Street shopping. The ease and convenience of Internet shopping may spell the end for many town as well as village High Streets. The recent closure of many Post Offices is a dismal reminder of how fragile trusted institutions have become in the twenty first century. Post Offices, which were once seen as essential to a community's well-being, are no longer needed in our virtual world.

Fortrose is currently fighting to preserve its High Street and a public meeting held mid 2013 demonstrated the depth of public feeling. There has been a proposal to build a new, larger, Co-operative Store with more car parking space plus other retail outlets, to create a retail park on the outskirts of Fortrose on a green field site opposite the school playing fields.

Fortrose High Street Mid Century

The traditional village trade and craft skills may be long gone but there will always be goods for sale and individuals making their living serving the needs of their community even though it may take unexpected forms like the Internet shopping on 'Ebay' or the 'House of Bruar' type of total experience for the leisure shopper, rather than the High Street we have known and loved in the past.

Source Material

First Statistical Account 1791
Rosemarkie Parish: Rosemarkie and Chanonry
Merchants 7, shoemakers and apprentices, 32, linen weavers 35, square wrights 4, mill wrights 2, tailors 4, masons 2, glovers 2, smith 1, butchers 2, writer 1, teachers, 4 minister1.

1901 Census, also recorded but gave no precise location:
Fortrose: Duncan McFee, butcher; High Street; Donald Ross, shoemaker; John Ross, shoemaker, Alexander Mackenzie, tailor; Castle Street; George Davidson, shoemaker, Union Street; Donald Macdonald, Shoemaker, Academy Street.
Rosemarkie: Alexander Sinclair, grocer; Gregory Kemp, Innkeeper, Kemps Lane; Roderick Mackenzie, butcher.

1911 Slater's Trade Directory exact location not known:
Fortrose: John Fraser, tailor, Station Road; John Goodlad, watchmaker; Michael Home, blacksmith, Shore; John Mackenzie, watchmaker, High Street; Roderick McKinnon, butcher; Miss Margaret Williamson, dressmaker; Neil Wilson, plumber.

North Star adverts 1930s; location not known
Fortrose: Taylor and son, Carpenters and Undertakers, West End; Market gardens growing fruit and vegetables: Bill Fulton, Precincts Road; Isa Ross's father, vegetable nursery.
Rosemarkie: Robert Watson, butcher.

Valuation Rolls Exact location of shops not known,
Fortrose:
1909 John Goodlad, watchmaker, High Street; Neil Wilson, plumber, Academy Street;
Rosemarkie: Alex Sinclair, merchant.

1911 Fortrose:
Alex Watson, barber, West End; George Sutherland, tailor, High Street; Thomas Fraser, tailor, The Shore; Robert Home, blacksmith and cycle agent, The Shore; Simon Macpherson, watchmaker, Viewfield Place; Mackenzie Alexander, tailor, West End; John Fraser, tailor, Academy Street; Mrs White, photographic studio, Castle Street; William Davidson, painter, High Street; Simon Ross Nelson, watchmaker, High Street;
Rosemarkie: Daniel Wilson, plumber.

1914 Rosemarkie: Robert Singer, tailor; Alexander Sinclair, grocer; Alexander Mackenzie and son, Alexander, master tailor and journeyman, Fortrose station.

1938/9 Fortrose: Neil Wilson, plumber; Simon Nelson, watchmaker; John Mackenzie, watchmaker ; Alex Mackenzie, The Cross; Wm Davidson, painter; Mrs White, photographic studio; John Fraser, tailor.

1955/6 Fortrose: Alex Mackeddie, painter, High Street; William Mackenzie, painter, High Street.

1982 shopping survey of Fortrose by G.P.Willis: chemist, bank, newsagent, baker/grocer, grocer (2), hardware store, draper, post office, café, shoemaker, and hairdresser.

Bibliography

Census 1881, 1901, 1911

Inland Revenue Survey 1911

North Star, A guide to Fortrose and Rosemarkie, 1930

Ross-shire Journal adverts from the 1930s

Slater's Trade Directory, 1903, 1911

Statistical Accounts, 1791, 1834, 1982

Valuation Rolls 1909/10,1911/14; 1931/39; 1942/3, 1945/6, 1950/51, 1955/56, 1960/61, 1971/72, 1985/86, 1995/96

S. Baron, ***A History of Shops and Shopping in Scotland***

F. Bassindale, ***Rosemarkie People and Places***

L. Bensley, ***The Village Shop***

S. Edmond, ***A Short History of the Parish of Fortrose and Rosemarkie***

Inverness Field Club, ***The Hub of the Highlands***

L.A.Lenney, ***The Historic Shop Fronts of Perth***

I.R.M. Mowat, ***Easter Ross 1750-1850***

D.R. Mills, ***Rural Community History from Trade Directories***

D. Willis, ***The Black Isle***